T0209461

DIVINE POSITIONING FOR A POWERFUL PURPOSE

Sheena Holbrooks

WESTBOW
P R E S S®
A DIVISION OF THOMAS NELSON
& ZONDERVAN

This book is a work of non-fiction. Unless otherwise noted, the author
and the publisher make no explicit guarantees as to the accuracy of
the information contained in this book and in some cases, names of
people and places have been altered to protect their privacy.

WestBow Press books may be ordered through booksellers or by contacting:

WestBow Press
A Division of Thomas Nelson & Zondervan
1663 Liberty Drive
Bloomington, IN 47403
www.westbowpress.com
1 (866) 928-1240

Because of the dynamic nature of the Internet, any web addresses or
links contained in this book may have changed since publication and
may no longer be valid. The views expressed in this work are solely those
of the author and do not necessarily reflect the views of the publisher,
and the publisher hereby disclaims any responsibility for them.

Any people depicted in stock imagery provided by Getty Images are
models, and such images are being used for illustrative purposes only.
Certain stock imagery © Getty Images.

Scripture taken from the New King James Version. Copyright © 1979, 1980,
1982 by Thomas Nelson, Inc. Used by permission. All rights reserved.

ISBN: 978-1-9736-7094-0 (sc)
ISBN: 978-1-9736-7095-7 (hc)
ISBN: 978-1-9736-7093-3 (e)

Library of Congress Control Number: 2019910885

Print information available on the last page.

WestBow Press rev. date: 09/11/2019

This Bible study is dedicated to all of those who inspired me to find my purpose in this life. To Kristi Lee for helping me edit this Bible study and to my husband Tim who saw my worth before I did; Thank you.

Contents

"God never said the journey would be easy, but he did say the journey would be worth while."- Max Lucado

Foreword

A few years ago, I got really sick. I went into Anaphylaxis in a store with no history of prior allergic reactions. I was able to inject epinephrine and get to the hospital, but it was one of the most terrifying experiences of my life. After that day, my body started to completely reject all foods and I couldn't be around (or use) any chemicals. This included shampoo, air fresheners, or cooking certain foods. The doctors had no clue what was wrong with me and I thought I was going to die.

Several weeks after that event, my liver started failing and my heart kept registering an abnormal EKG. I couldn't go to work and I needed help just to walk to my mailbox. I said to God, "I would rather lose a leg than deal with this." Immediately, God responded and said, "Do not wish for a permanent solution to a temporary problem." That word from God gave me the motivation to get better and to heal my body, mind and my spirit.

For the last eighteen months, I have been solely focused on self-restoration. I have dedicated my time to understanding the importance of faith, patience and Godly positioning. I wanted to share some of the things I have learned through my journey; to inspire women to keep going. God has a reason for our situations, we just have to find the purpose in it.

My healing journey may end up being a life-long commitment but without God reshaping my life from the ground up, I would never have grown in a way that has given me such a love for people, and a genuinely positive outlook on life. I may always have doctors on speed dial, but these bodies are temporary anyway. The state of our souls are what truly matter. The soul lasts for eternity.

I hope that you are blessed as you read this Bible study and that these daily reminders inspire you to keep up your faith. As a follower of Christ, you are exactly where God intended you to be.

1

Eve: The Original Sin
Genesis 3:1-7

Eve is perhaps the most famous woman in history. She was the first woman, created from Adam's rib to be a companion to him, and she was the first person to fall for the devil's deceptions. When we read the story of Adam and Eve, we must remember that the devil was once an angel. He knows how to manipulate us.

When Eve decided to eat the fruit, she wasn't doing so out of open rebellion. Sin was not known to Adam and Eve at that time. Satan painted the act of eating the fruit as okay, and Eve was deceived into believing that it was good.

This is why prayer is so important. Not everything that is harmful to us is easily recognized. Even the best of intentions can lead to sin. But, through prayer, we can become more in-tune with the Holy Spirit's guidance (Luke 12:12, 1 Corinthians 2:10-12).

After Adam and Eve ate the fruit, they lost their innocence. They realized they were naked and wanted to be covered. They hid from God because they knew there would be consequences for their actions, but God didn't turn his back on them. Instead, he helped them make clothes to cover their bodies. While they still had to deal with the outcome of their decisions, God never left them to pick up the pieces on their own.

I don't think it was by mistake that the devil went after Eve first. The man may be the head of the household, but the woman generally has influence to change her husband's mind. Satan knew that by getting Eve to eat the fruit first, she would be able to convince Adam to follow suit. We must be very careful where we are guiding our husbands and how we are influencing them. Our words and actions affect the entire family. We should build our homes with a strong foundation that is steadfast and unmovable (Ephesians 4:14).

> "The wise woman builds her house, but the foolish tears it down with her hands." Proverbs 14:1

2

Delilah: The Price of Greed
Judges 16:15-18

The story of Delilah begins with Samson. Samson was a Nazarite who abandoned God's calling on his life when he met Delilah. He became infatuated with her. The book of Judges clearly states that he fell in love with her, but it never mentions that those feelings were reciprocated.

Samson had great strength that no man could match, and the secret to his strength was in his hair. When Philistine rulers became aware of their relationship, they tempted Delilah with money to betray Samson in order to find out the source of his incredible strength.

Delilah eventually seduced Samson. He told her that if his hair was cut, he would become weak. Delilah quickly told the Philistines what she had learned, and they cut his hair. Samson lost his strength and was easily subdued. Delilah was paid, and the Philistines thought they had won.

However, Samson's hair grew back. During a pagan festival, Samson was chained and put on display as a sign of victory. It was in that moment that his strength returned. Samson brought down an entire building and destroyed more of God's enemies in that one night than he had in his entire life.

Delilah may have been a Philistine, but I don't think her blood money came without consequence. Statistics show that those with higher incomes are 4.5 percent more likely to commit suicide from the stress related to their riches. Another statistic showed that 70 percent of lottery winners become bankrupt.

In Matthew 19:24, Jesus said, "It is easier for a camel to pass through the eye of a needle than for a rich man to enter the Kingdom of God." While there is nothing wrong with wealth, and God wants us to be blessed, the way in which we acquire wealth needs to be examined.

Wealth achieved by questionable means will not be blessed by God. You may not have destroyed someone's life for financial gain like Delilah did, but have you traded your time with God for extra shifts at work? Have you ever looked the other way when something seemed morally controversial because you knew you would benefit from the outcome?

We must be vigilant and make sure we are not getting in the habit of putting our souls on the back burner for riches. Our lives are no more than a vapor that is only seen for a moment before it is gone (James 4:14). This world is not our home. While God wants to see us prosper here on earth, it is not meant to be a permanent residence.

We cannot take our money with us when we leave this world. We must be careful not to sacrifice our souls for financial gain or through the means in which we acquire it.

"For the love of money, is the root of all evil." 1 Timothy 6:10

References:

1. http://business.time.com/2012/11/08/why-suicides-are-more-common-in-richer-neighborhoods/
2. https://brandongaille.com/22-lottery-winners-bankrupt-statistics/

3

Potiphar's Wife #1:
Consequences of Revenge
Genesis 39:11-18

The story of Potiphar's wife begins with Joseph. Joseph was Jacob's favorite son. His jealous brothers took him to Egypt to be sold as a slave. The man who bought Joseph was named Potiphar. He was a high-ranking official and captain of the guard. Joseph's character won him favor in the eyes of Potiphar, who put Joseph in charge of his entire house.

The story changes when Potiphar's wife tries to seduce Joseph. On three different occasions, she approached Joseph, and he turned her down. Out of anger, she told her husband that Joseph had forced himself on her. Potiphar became jealous and sent Joseph to prison.

Have you ever been in a situation that you felt was unfair and you wanted to take matters into your own hands? Did the idea of seeking revenge on someone cross your mind? Maybe you even went through with it and then quickly realized there is no lasting joy in revenge.

Potiphar's wife may have felt like she won in the moment, but she had to live with the realization that she had a man thrown in prison while seeking her own vengeance. Romans 12:19 says, "Beloved, do not avenge yourselves, but rather give place to wrath; for it is written, 'Vengeance is Mine, I will repay,' says the Lord."

Seeking retribution causes us to feel resentment and bitterness. Our minds end up becoming consumed with destructive thoughts about another human being. This unresolved anger and animosity will have a negative impact on our spiritual lives, and on our physical bodies.

In Hebrews 12:15, the Bible says, "Looking carefully lest anyone fall short of the grace of God; lest any root of bitterness springing up cause trouble, and by this many, become defiled." The word *defile* means to poison, infect, or corrupt; and anything that happens in the spiritual will eventually bleed over into the physical. Take care of yourself. Let go of any bitterness you're holding onto.

> "See that no one renders evil for evil to anyone, but always pursue what is good both for yourself and for all."1 Thessalonians 5:15

4

Potiphar's Wife #2:
Poisonous Thoughts
Philippians 4:6-8

Today I want to expand a little more on how important it is to protect our minds and be aware of our thoughts.

Depression, unexplained illness, and body pain can all be the result of mental and emotional stress. When we dwell on the negative aspects of our past, we get stuck there and it starts to affect all aspects of our bodies.

Proverbs 23:7 says, "For as he thinks in his heart, so is he." Thoughts of revenge lead to corrupting our roots. Corrupting our roots leads to physical and spiritual problems simultaneously. We cannot draw closer to God and wish ill will toward someone. Choose today who you will serve, because no one can have two masters (Joshua 24:15, Matthew 6:24).

Will you satisfy your own need for vengeance, or will you allow God to rectify your past according to his will? People are known by their fruits. Will you be known as a vindictive person, or will you be known as a follower of Christ?

The Bible is very clear on what our thoughts should be focused on. In Philippians 4:8, God tells us that we are to think about things that are true, noble, just, pure, lovely, of good report, virtuous, and praise worthy. Taking matters into our own hands will only escalate the situation and cause us even more trouble. God knows the best way to handle the circumstances, and he takes care of his children. If you are one of God's children, he will handle it. We only have to trust him.

No matter how we feel about someone, God still loves that person. You will never meet a person God does not love.

> "That Christ may dwell in your hearts through faith; that you, being rooted and grounded in love, may be able to comprehend with all the saints what is the width and length and depth and height- to know the love of Christ which passes knowledge; that you may be filled with all the fullness of God." Ephesians 3:17-19

5

Jezebel: Gifts Gone Wrong
Matthew 7:18-21

Jezebel has been known throughout history as the embodiment of pure evil. She was brought up in a society that worshipped several gods. Among the most powerful was Ba'al. Jezebel lived a life of luxury in a very prominent household. When Ahab took Jezebel as his wife, he strayed from God and started to worship Ba'al with her. He allowed her to build several temples throughout Israel.

Jezebel hosted many pagan celebrations that involved ritual prostitution and eating foods that had been given in sacrifice. As her following grew, so did her power. She eventually started killing prophets of God to establish Ba'al as the true god of Israel. Jezebel is the first religious prosecutor in biblical history.

There is no doubt that Jezebel had God-given gifts (talents), but she chose to use them in the wrong manner. She was a natural leader, influential, and her lineage put her in a position of power. Jezebel could have done amazing things for the kingdom of God if her focus had shifted. She could have very well been revered as the next Deborah, but she is known throughout history as an immoral religious persecutor.

Jezebel was in a place to make a lasting difference. One that would have truly changed history. Instead, her lineage died off completely not long after her brutal death.

With any gift comes responsibility. We must be aware of our influence and be vigilant to maintain a walk with Christ that will not hinder others. When we use our talents for selfish gain, we are head down the same path that led to Jezebel's destruction.

We all have the capacity to make contributions to God's Kingdom through our talents. We are all born with a natural ability to be good at something. Whether we focus on that gift or not is up to us. Spiritual gifts are given to us through salvation.

When we profess Jesus as our savior, God gives each one of us a spiritual gift. These gifts consist of prophecy, serving, teaching, exhortation, giving, leadership, wisdom, faith, healing, miracles, discernment, pastoring, and mercy.

Gifts of the spirit are written several times in the New Testament, and the list varies each time. I believe Paul was referring to the spiritual gifts that were needed for each church he was talking to. More than likely, he didn't list all of them. I think the spiritual gifts that are essential manifest as the needs of the church do (1Corinthians 12:4). If we are diligent to use our spiritual gift the right way, God will bestow more on us to help further the Kingdom of God (1 Corinthians 12:31).

Sometimes we have a hard time figuring out what our gifts might be. They may not even seem like gifts to us. Does singing come naturally to you? Maybe you can speak eloquently in front of large crowds. Do you have a heart for children, or possibly prisoners? That passion is what will lead you to fulfill your God-given calling. Develop the talents you have and watch how God uses you to further his kingdom.

> "And whatever ye do, do it heartily, as to the Lord,
> and not to men." Colossians 3:23

6

Sapphira: Misplaced Loyalty
Acts 5:1-11

Sapphira and her husband Ananias were members of the first church. The Christians in the church were donating the money earned from selling some of their properties to the Apostles. Then, the Apostles would divide the money up to all of those in need.

When Ananias sold his property, he decided to keep most of the money. Peter confronted him about the money, and Ananias lied.

In Acts 5:3-4 Peter said to him, "Ananias, why has Satan filled your heart to lie to the Holy Spirit and keep back part of the price of the land for yourself? While it remained, was it not your own? And after it was sold, was it not in your own control? Why have you conceived this thing in your heart? You have not lied to men but to God."

The problem wasn't in keeping the money, it was lying about it. The money was his to do what he pleased, but he chose to deceive the church instead. Because of this, the Holy Spirit struck him dead on the spot.

A few hours later, Sapphira was confronted by Peter. He asked her if the money they had donated was all the money they had received from the sale. She protected her husband by perpetuating the lie and said, "Yes." In that moment, she was also struck down and died.

As women, we are to honor our significant others. We are to support them and stand beside them through trials. We are to be a team; a man respecting and cherishing his woman, and a woman respecting and honoring her man. But what happens when his ways go against God's ways?

Psalm 103:17-18 says," But the mercy of the Lord is from everlasting to everlasting on those who fear him, and his righteousness to children's children, to such as keep his covenant, and to those who remember his commandments to do them." Above all else, we are to honor God and obey him. God's laws will always trump honoring a spouse's conduct.

In return for that obedience, God offers us his lovingkindness (mercy). The Holy Spirit has been given to us to help guide us, but it isn't to be taken lightly. The Holy Spirit is God. Lying to the Holy Spirit is still lying to God, and the same consequences apply.

When Sapphira was standing in front of Peter, I wonder what thoughts were running through her head. She was a member of the first church and understood God's laws. In order to lie to the Holy Spirit, she must have felt some type of conviction and tried to justify her actions. Did she hesitate on lying? Or had she managed to convince herself it was acceptable, because she was protecting her husband?

We must be careful who we choose to enter life-long union with. If we choose men who are dishonest, we are going to be facing moral dilemmas like this often. The man we choose to marry should have a strong relationship with Jesus Christ and possess Godly character.

Character is not defined by the way we act in public, but by what we choose to do behind closed doors. The husband we choose needs to be in line with the God we are serving. Who are you choosing to honor today?

> "Let every soul be subject to the governing authorities. For there is no authority except from God, and the authorities that exist are appointed by God." Romans 13:1

7

Lot's Wife: Missing a Sinful Past
Genesis 19:15-29

Lot and his family lived in Sodom. Sodom was one of the two cities that God was about to destroy because of their wickedness. One night, God sent two angels to warn Lot of the destruction that was about to demolish the cities. In Genesis 19:17, they were told to escape for their lives and not look back.

Lot and his daughters obeyed and ran as fast as they could. They didn't look back, but Lot's wife did. As she mourned the loss of her old life, she was turned in to a pillar of salt. She was hesitant to obey God because of her attachment to her past (sinful) life. She loved her home in Sodom and she chose to grieve, instead of listening to God's command to run and not look back.

Not only was Lot's wife reminiscent of what she was losing, but she also blatantly disobeyed God. When we become Christians, we leave our old life behind.

We should never desire to be the person we were before Christ was part of our lives. If our lives were going so well, we wouldn't have felt the need for Jesus Christ. We knew we were missing something;

there was an emptiness. God freed us from a life of emptiness and gave us purpose.

2 Timothy 1:9 says, "Who has saved us and called us with a holy calling, not according to our works, but according to His own purpose and grace which was given to us in Christ Jesus before time began." Striving to fulfill that calling on our lives, is what we were made for.

Being a Christian gives us an advantage we didn't have before we were saved. We have God in our corner. He gives us the answers we seek, makes sure our needs are met, and blesses us beyond measure (John 1:16).

As our creator, God knows us better than we know ourselves. He knows exactly what we need. Giving God control of our lives and letting him design our future will give us peace and fulfillment. He isn't trying to take things away, but he is trying to protect us. Sin only satisfies for a season, but God brings lasting contentment.

"Remember Lot's Wife" Luke 17:32

8

Esther: The Orphan Queen
Esther 4:12-17

The women in the Bible are nothing short of amazing. They personify what most of us strive to be daily. Esther was no exception and she was positioned by God for one defining moment. One moment that required an ultimate act of bravery.

Esther was a beautiful Jewish orphan. She won a beauty pageant to become queen. Once she had settled into her new life in the palace, she heard of a scheme from Haman to kill all the Jews. Haman was the king's highest advisor, and she knew that his word held weight. When Esther was made aware of his plans, she organized a feast for the king and Haman.

During the feast, she risked her life to tell the king the truth about her lineage and Haman's plans of genocide. Death could have been an immediate punishment for her, but she trusted God with her life and stepped out of her comfort zone. The king listened to her and sentenced Haman to death for his terrible plans. Esther's faith was rewarded, and she saved the Jewish people.

As an orphan, Esther would have dealt with insecurity, self-esteem issues, and a passive demeanor. Essentially, she had to cope with an identity crisis. In order to do what God called her to do, she had to figure out who she was. Once she did, she was able to be the woman God intended her to be. She realized that she was the daughter of the God and developed the confidence needed to fulfill her destiny.

We cannot step into our destinies until we learn who we are and believe it. It is not enough to know we are fearless, powerful women. We must embody that with confidence as well. You may have not even noticed the orphan spirit operating in your own life, because it is not a spirit that is brought about by sin. It is one that is developed during adolescents through a lack of protection and provision from earthly fathers.

People who deal with this spirit feel a constant sense of abandonment. They suffer from a lack of self-worth that tends to cloud their minds consistently. Do you ever feel alone, even when you're not? Do you tend reject people before they can reject you? Do you sabotage relationships in fear of getting too close? Do you feel like you're just not good enough?

John 14:18, Jesus says, "I will not leave you orphans, I will come to you." God has a very specific purpose for you in this life; a purpose designed just for you.

If you reach out to Him, He will help you gain the self-worth needed to defeat this orphan spirit and become exactly who He intended you to be.

> "Being confident of this very thing, that he who begun a good work in you will complete it until the day of Jesus Christ." Phil. 1:6

9

Deborah: A Fearless Warrior
Judges 4:4-10

Deborah was a biblical superhero. She was a judge, a prophetess, motivator, military strategist, and a poet. She was an Incredible warrior on and off the battlefield. Her inspirational speeches rallied troops to fight against insurmountable odds and win!

Her faith in God gave her the confidence to see through the most difficult of battles with grace and purpose. The call on Deborah's life was huge, and she became one of the most influential people in the Bible. She did not allow fear to prevent her from being everything God had called her to be.

It is easy to become overwhelmed when we see the magnitude of the calling that God has placed on our lives. However, it is important to remember that God's call on our lives is progressive. It takes time to fulfill. Deborah was a middle-aged woman before she fulfilled her calling. You will have the training, experience, and skills needed to fulfill your purpose when the time comes.

We have a habit of looking at ourselves through timid glasses. We see what is right in front of us, and nothing else. We see ourselves as unqualified, while God sees us very differently.

Women have played a prominent role in developing God's kingdom since the beginning. The goal of this Bible study is to show the importance of women in the ministry. God does not discriminate when it comes to sharing the Gospel of Jesus. If it weren't for the women who fulfilled their purpose and inspired me, I would never have found my voice.

A year ago, I prayed and asked God to show me how he sees me. He immediately told me I was strong, confident, and powerful. I have used strong to define myself over the years, but never confident or powerful. To see myself the way God saw me, changed my life. I realized the true power behind verses like Phil. 4:13. I realized that I could do anything through Christ, and I was the only one holding me back.

Take a moment today and ask God how he sees you, and let that define who you are.

"For I know the thoughts that I think towards you, says the Lord. Thoughts of peace and not of evil, to give you an expected end." Jeremiah 29:11

10

Rahab: A Clean Slate
Joshua 6:22-25
Psalms 103:12-13

Rahab was a prostitute and inn keeper in Jericho. Her story begins when she hid two Israelite spies on the roof of her inn. The king heard of the spies and sent his own men to Rahab's home to kill them. She lied to the soldiers and sent them in the opposite direction.

After the soldiers left, Rahab confessed to the Israelite spies that she knew the Lord had given them the land where Jericho stood (Joshua 2:9). In return for hiding the spies, Rahab asked that her household be saved when the Israelites infiltrated Jericho. They honored her wish and protected her family. Rahab converted to Judaism and married Salmon. She became the grandmother of Boaz and part of the lineage of Jesus Christ himself.

The Bible does not explain how Rahab knew of the Lord as a Canaanite, but it does mention that she had heard of his miracles (Joshua 2:10). Being an inn keeper, Rahab would have heard stories from many different lands. I believe as some of these travelers shared stories of Moses, she felt conviction for the first time. God gently spoke to her heart. She had a God-given purpose, even as a Canaanite prostitute. (Ephesians 1:17-18)

Rahab is relatable to me. I was not a prostitute, but I was a drug addict. One night in 2011, I had over-dosed and I was alone when it happened. By the grace of God, I woke up at some point in the night. I realized that I could have died in that bathroom. It could have been weeks before anyone even knew. I didn't have any real friends to check on me, or any local family.

It was at that moment I hit my crossroads. I could continue the path I was on and ultimately lose my life, or I could make a change. I called out to God and he answered. I grew up in church, but it wasn't until that moment that I was truly saved. I realized God had never left me. He was right there waiting for me to reach out to him.

When God rescued me that night, my past didn't matter. He gave me a clean slate, just like Rahab (Hebrews 10:17).

None of us are prisoners of our past. Once we are saved, we are free from who we once were. God isn't focused on the old self, he is only focused on the person we are becoming. God saw a former prostitute fit for the lineage of Jesus Christ because of her faith, and willingness to lay down her life for the Truth.

The mess that God brings us out of is our testimony. It is what God will use to fulfill our callings. We inspire others through our own struggles. 2 Corinthians 5:17 says, "Anyone who belongs to Christ has become a new person. The old life is gone; a new life has begun." We get a new life when we are born again in Christ Jesus. We get freedom and purpose.

> "If we confess our sins, he is faithful and just to forgive
> us our sins and purify us from all unrighteousness."
> 1 John 1:9

11

Jael: Taking Down Giants
Judges 4:17-21

The story of Jael begins in the time of Deborah. When Deborah was at the peak of her calling, Jael was unheard of. From the scriptures we are given, Jael was an average woman with no special talents or skills. She was the wife of Heber and her people were at peace with the Canaanites during the war with the Israelites.

Sisera was the leader of the Canaanite army. When the Israelites were winning the battle, he fled on foot and he ended up at the tent of Jael. Because of the peace between their lands, Sisera felt safe to seek shelter there. Jael took care of him and he eventually fell asleep. At that point, Jael took a tent peg and a hammer and killed him. This act was the beginning of the end for the Canaanite reign.

The next morning, Jael found the leader of the Israelite army and showed him Sisera. Deborah celebrated Jael's actions by writing a song about her. She referred to Jael as, "Most blessed of all women" (Judges 5:24).

Jael didn't take down the leader of this great army with a sword but with items she had available. She used a tent peg and a hammer. She was not trained in combat, nor did she have a soldier's weapon, but God made sure she had what she needed to fulfill her destiny. If she had had a sword or military training, Sisera might not have let his guard down. He may have sought another tent to seek asylum in. It was all in God's perfect design that Jael was a warrior, without the appearance of such.

God doesn't always choose the one most qualified to fulfill his will. Jael was available and willing. That was all it took for God to use her to help God's people win the battle. Romans 8:28 says, "And we know that all things work together for good to them that love God, to those that are called according to his purpose." We don't need to be college graduates, professional athletes, or mega-church pastors to be used. All we need to be is willing.

> "And God is able to make all grace abound toward you, always having sufficiency in all things, may have an abundance for every good work." 2 Corinthians 9:8

12

Tamar: Fearless Determination
Genesis 38:20-26

There are three different women named Tamar in the Bible. Two of them were abused by close family members, and their stories were tragic. The third Tamar was a story of determination.

This Tamar was married to Judah's son, Er. Er died suddenly before he could give her any children. By law, Judah's second son Onan, was supposed to give her an heir that would be considered Er's offspring. When he refused to give her a child, God struck him down and he also died suddenly.

Judah had one more son, but he was too young to marry. Judah promised that when Shelah was of age, Judah would let them marry. However, Judah never followed through with his promise.

In order to reclaim her place in Judah's family, Tamar devises a plan for Judah to impregnate her. She sat outside the gates and waited for him to return from a festival. Judah propositioned her and promised her a goat as payment. He gave Tamar his staff as a sign of good faith and left

Soon, the news of Tamar's pregnancy started to spread, and Judah was determined to maintain his honor. He said that Tamar should be burned alive for not remaining faithful to his family. Before he could go through with this punishment, Tamar gave him back his staff and let him know that she was pregnant with his twin boys.

Judah publicly acknowledged her innocence and said in Genesis 38:26, "She has been more righteous than I." Essentially, he was feeling guilty for not allowing Tamar to give birth to his heir. Because of her determination, Jesus became one of her descendants.

Most of us have been rejected or turned down at some point in our lives. Maybe you didn't get the job you applied for, or maybe you weren't chosen for the lead role in a play. Rejection hurts, but it isn't always a bad thing. Sometimes it is just a redirection. We must keep going towards the goal and seek God's direction. (Phil 3:14).

Tamar kept pressing forward no matter how many times she was told no. She knew what God had promised her and didn't stop until that purpose was fulfilled in her life. God has a plan for all of us, and he also has a specific way for us to implement that plan. If we hear no, it doesn't mean that we heard God wrong, it means that there is a different avenue in which his plan for us will be better completed. We just have to keep going.

"I have fought the good fight, I have finished the course, I have kept the faith." 2 Timothy 4:7

13

Jehosheba:
Unparalleled Bravery
2 Chronicles 22:11
2 Kings 11:2

When King Ahaziah died, his mother Athaliah made herself queen and ordered that anyone who could claim the throne be executed. When her daughter Jehosheba learned of the execution, she took her nephew Joash and hid him in the temple until he was old enough to claim the throne for himself.

Six years later when Joash was just seven years old, he was sworn in as king and Athaliah was put to death. This one act of bravery preserved the lineage of David, who was an ancestor of Jesus Christ.

Athaliah was the daughter of Jezebel and broke the alliance between the northern and southern kingdoms when she became queen by promoting Ba'al worship just as her mother had. When Joash became king, the people celebrated by destroying the temples of Ba'al.

This courageous aunt prevented the extinction of the Davidic Line. How many times throughout Biblical history have we seen the blood line of Jesus Christ attacked? Yet God's plan always prevails. Jehosheba was positioned exactly where God wanted her to protect her nephew. She was fearless and brave. She did the right thing in the face of opposition and God's people prevailed because she believed.

Sometimes we feel out of place and question our purpose. But as children of God, we must be confident in our Lord and realize he knows exactly what he is doing (Proverbs 3:26). We cannot see farther than what is in front of us with natural eyes, and that is where faith comes in to play. When we only focus on the natural, we lose sight of the truth.

We may see a job loss and feel the stress of a family to support, but God said he will provide all our needs if we seek him first (Matthew 6:33). It may look hopeless to us, but God has a plan in place. Jehosheba didn't let the mass execution of her family members deter her from fulfilling her purpose. She stepped into an impossible situation and saved Joash. She knew God was with her, and His will would prevail.

Let's try to embody Jehosheba's confidence and see our circumstances through The Word of God (spiritual eyes). If God said it, it will happen, but we must have faith. God knows what he is doing, and he has chosen us to play a role in furthering his kingdom.

> "Paul, a bondservant of God and an apostle of Jesus Christ according to the faith of God's elect and their acknowledgement of the truth which accords with godliness, in hope of eternal life, which God, who cannot lie, promised before time began." Titus 1:1-2

14

Miriam: When Complacency Takes Root
Numbers 12:1-10

Miriam played a huge role in keeping Moses safe and eventually freeing the Israelites. When the story of Moses begins among the reeds, we see Miriam show bravery and wit. She cleverly positioned her mother to nurse Moses for the Pharaoh's daughter. She was very young to possess such qualities. These were the traits of a true leader in the making!

When Moses finally freed the Hebrew slaves from Egypt, Miriam was by his side leading the women (Exodus 2:20-21). The Bible refers to her as a prophetess. A prophet is someone who God communicates to directly. God had chosen Miriam to speak through.

Somewhere along the way, Miriam became complacent. She wasn't happy with the way her younger brother was leading Israelites, and she began to complain. A woman in her position was very influential, and she could have deterred some of the women from following God based on her attitude alone. She gossiped to her brother Aaron who started to despise Moses' leadership as well.

In Numbers 12:2, Miriam said to Aaron, "Has the Lord indeed

only spoken through Moses? Has he not spoken through us also?" Her gossiping had bred jealousy over Moses' position. Motivated by pride, she tore down the man God had placed in authority over her. God was unhappy with Miriam's actions, and she was struck down with leprosy.

As Miriam sought more authority, God quickly reminded her that he could take it all away. Even knowing what his sister had done, Moses cried out to God on her behalf for her healing and God answered. After seven days, the leprosy disappeared.

There is a hierarchy that has been established by God. Church leaders are to be revered and respected. If they are in the will of God, we are to support them.

In a marriage, the man is the head of the household. Do you have a hard time following your husband's lead? What about your boss? To dishonor those in authority is to dishonor God. The Bible says that the tongue can defile the entire body (James 3:6). It contains the power of life and death (Proverbs 8:21). The words we choose, shape who we are.

Are you going to use that power to edify and serve those in authority, or are you going to deter them? Gossip is a gateway to dissention. Let's encourage each other and help those God has placed over us fulfill their purposes as well.

> "And the tongue is a fire, a world of iniquity. The tongue is so set among our members that it defiles the whole body, and sets on fire the course of nature, and it is set on fire by hell." James 3:6

15

Dinah #1: Soul Ties
Genesis chapter 34:1-4
Ephesians 5:25-31

Dinah was the youngest daughter of Jacob and Leah. She wasn't much different than an average teenage girl in our society today. Dinah was social, and enjoyed spending her time with, "the other daughters of the land" (Genesis 34:1). On one particular day, she caught the eye of Prince Shechem. Genesis 34:2 states that Shechem took her, laid with her, and defiled her. In other words, he raped her.

The Bible doesn't give us a narrative from Dinah's point of view after this event, but I can imagine she felt quite degraded and even ashamed. Despite being violated in this manner, Shechem falls in love with her, "And his soul was strongly attracted to Dinah" (Genesis 34:3). Their encounter formed a soul tie.

A soul tie connects two people in the spiritual realm, through a physical means. It is a deep bond that is meant to be shared between a husband and a wife. Several times in the Bible, God uses the phrase, "to become one flesh." He is reaffirming the importance of such a bond. Sexual relations will knit our souls with another person. We need to be very selective who we share our souls with.

Our culture treats sex as a social norm, that it is just a way to fulfill a physical desire. However, as we see through Scripture, it is much more than that. It is a way to connect to our spouses and form a tight-knit bond. Unhealthy and abusive relationships will almost always have premature sexual relations in common.

We become bound to someone who isn't right for us, and it makes it that much harder to break free from them. It can also cause us to turn a blind eye to their actions and to justify their behavior.

Soul ties can be formed in other ways as well. Whenever we are sharing a significant amount of our time, or energy with someone, we will eventually form a similar connection with them. If we are not careful, it can lead to the creation of bad habits. We become who we spend our time with.

"Evil company corrupts good habits."
1 Cor. 15:33

16

Dinah #2: Breaking Soul Ties
Psalm 118:5
Mark 11:22-24
2 Corinthians 3:17

Yesterday we discussed how soul ties were formed. Today we will go over how we can break these unhealthy connections. God has given us freedom from these bonds through Jesus Christ, and we are not doomed to suffer the consequences of ill-fated relationships. God's healing is not just for physical ailments, but for strongholds in our minds, and souls as well.

Cutting off communication and throwing away mementos is the first step in this healing process. We can become emotionally invested in physical objects, and these physical objects are reminders of the person we are trying to free ourselves from.

Keeping these items will only continue to reestablish the connection. This step can become complicated if children are the connection between two people, but freedom is still possible.

The next step is forgiveness. Forgiving the other person does not unencumber them from the consequences of their actions, but it frees us from being burdened by their presence in our minds. This process can take time depending on how strong the soul tie is.

Don't forget to forgive yourself as well. We can sometimes harbor unnecessary guilt from these relationships, but God does not want us carrying this burden. God is love and his perfect love cast out all fear. There is no condemnation in Christ Jesus (1 John 4:18, Roman 8:1).

Once forgiveness is possible, we must verbalize it. Biblically speaking, the power of life and death are in the tongue (Proverbs 18:21). Speaking out and claiming the severed soul tie will finalize it.

We have all made bad decisions in our past, but the past is not who we are, and we can take control of our future starting today. We can become who we are in Christ Jesus if we accept the gift of freedom that he has given to us, through his sacrifice on Calvary.

> "Therefore, if anyone is in Christ, he is a new creation; old, all things have passed away; behold all things have become new!" 2 Cor. 5:17

17

Woman with the Issue of Blood #1: Faith in Action Mark 5:25-34

The Woman with the Issue of Blood has been my main focus this past year. After developing several auto immune conditions, I was looking for a healing. This woman had spent all her money on doctors who could not help her, and she was only getting worse.

In her desperation, she sought out Jesus after hearing about his miracles. She pushed through the crowd just to reach out and touch his clothes. She believed that if she could just touch the hem of his garment, she would be healed. And that is exactly what happened. Her faith healed her (Mark 5:34).

On my darkest days, I would replay this story in my mind to give myself hope. I didn't understand why God wasn't snapping his fingers and restoring my body. I mean, I try to do the right thing every day. I read my Bible, I take my family to church, and I share the love of Jesus with people. So, why did this happen to me?

Before I got sick, I was in the gym four days a week, over booking my kid's schedules, and still trying to maintain a social life. God didn't exactly fit in to that life. I loved Jesus, but we were just too busy. I was exhausted, anxious, and mentally drained. I was a mess! It wasn't until God hit the reset button with my entire life, that I was able to rebuild it again from the bottom up.

When I got sick, I was able to focus on spending time with God. Over the course of the next year, I realized my entire family was more relaxed, happier, and healthier. Even though I am still fighting my way back with chronic illness, I am more at peace than I have ever been in my life. Most of the time I can live in the present with patience, and that alone was worth everything I went through.

God would never have been able to truly reach me if he didn't force me to slow down. Our bodies are fragile. They were not meant to last forever, but our souls are. The state of our souls is much more important than our physical bodies. If an illness gets us right with God, then it was a blessing.

The Woman with the Issue of Blood was healed because she trusted God. Her faith changed her entire life, but it was her sickness that gave her, her testimony. We must trust God enough to know that he will heal us, but it will be in his time not ours.

> "For our light affliction, which is but for a moment, is working for us a far more exceeding and eternal weight of glory, while we do not look at the things which are seen, but at the things which are not seen. For the things which are seen are temporary, but the things which are not seen are eternal." 2 Corinthians 4:17-18

18

Woman with the Issue of Blood #2: Healing with Patience
Mark 11:24
1 Peter 5:10

Healing is not a quick fix. True restoration is a total overhaul of our mental, emotional, and physical beings. It does not happen in an instant. God is patient. As humans, there are certain things we must endure to learn (Hebrews 12:1).

Through my life experiences, I am now able to relate to drug addicts, abused women (PTSD sufferers), single moms, and chronically ill/disabled people. If it wasn't for my pain, I would never have understood their struggles. If God fixed me immediately, I would never have been able to show God's love to so many factions of people and relate to them. There is always purpose in our pain.

God can heal us. God wants to heal us. There are over 50 scriptures that I have found about healing. If God did not want us to be healed, I can assure you he would not have spoken about it so much. God's love for us surpasses understanding (Eph. 3:19). He only wants what is best for us.

When I try to grasp the depth of God's love for us, I think of the love I have for my own children. When I make them do chores or take things away from them, it is to help them grow and learn. God is doing the same thing with us. Philippians 4:6-7 says, " Be anxious for nothing, but in everything by prayer and supplication, with thanksgiving, let your requests be made known to God; and the peace of God, which surpasses all understanding, will guard your hearts and minds through Christ Jesus."

As children of God, we have access to that peace. A peace that transcends understanding! Regardless of what we are going through, we can be at peace about it.

He is going to take care of everything. God will heal all of us.

> "I waited patiently for the LORD; and he inclined to me and heard my cry. He also brought me up out of a horrible pit, out of the miry clay, and set my feet upon a rock, and established my steps. He has put a new song in my mouth. Praise to our God; many will see it and fear, and will trust in the LORD." Psalms 40:1-3

19

Martha: Refocus
Luke 10:38-42

Martha is an individual we can all relate to. As women, we are constantly preparing things, keeping schedules, cleaning, cooking, and making sure everyone is taken care of. Amid this, it is easy for us to become overwhelmed and lose sight of what is important, just like Martha did.

In Luke 10, Jesus had gone to visit Mary and Martha in Bethany. Martha was determined to be the best hostess she possibly could be, while Mary decided to sit down and listen to Jesus speak.

Irritated by the amount of work she was doing on her own, Martha became hyper-focused on Mary. She felt that Mary should have been helping her with all the household duties. In Luke 10:40-42, Martha finally hit her breaking point. She confronted Jesus and said, "Do you not care that my sister has left me to do all this work by myself? Tell her to help me!"

Jesus saw her heart and replied, "Martha, you are worried and upset about many things. Only one thing is important. Mary has chosen the better thing, and it will never be taken away from her."

It is so easy to get caught up in the day to day that we forget what our true purpose is. We end up living in a constant state of stress trying to keep up with appointments, practices, diets, exercise, and maintaining some semblance of a personal life. This leaves us high strung, and with no peace in our hearts.

Sometimes we just need to sit down and listen to Jesus speak to us before we get caught up in a perpetual cycle of negativity. 2 Corinthians 10:5 says to take captive every thought to the obedience of Christ. If we notice a destructive line of thought generating in our minds, we are commanded to change our thinking and focus on the right things (Philippians 2:14).

God had given us a way out when we are tempted to dwell on the negative. He will never tempt us beyond what we can handle (1 Corinthians 10:13).

"And let the peace of God rule in your hearts, to which you were also called in one body, and be thankful." Colossians 3:15

20

Jochebed and Pharaoh's Daughter: Two Worlds, One Purpose
Exodus 2:5-10

The story of these two unlikely women begins with Moses. When Pharaoh had seen that the Israelite numbers had grown substantially, he became concerned with an uprising. He ordered all the Hebrew boys to be thrown into the Nile river.

In order to protect her son, Moses' mother Jochebed, placed him in a basket among the reeds of the Nile. Moses' sister Miriam kept an eye on the basket from a distance.

When Pharaoh's daughter came across the baby boy, she felt sorry for him. Miriam asked the Egyptian princess if she would like her to find a Hebrew woman to nurse him. In Exodus 2:9, Pharaoh's daughter said, "Take this child away and nurse him for me, and I will give you wages."

Miriam returned Moses to his mother, and Pharaoh's daughter paid her to nurse him. Under the Egyptian's protection, Jochebed was able to raise her son for several years until he returned to the palace to live.

When Pharaoh ordered the babies to be killed, I can only imagine the fear that Jochebed felt. She may have questioned God and been angry with him, but she remained faithful. God put Pharaoh's daughter exactly where she needed to be and filled her heart with compassion for Moses. In a situation the seemed hopeless, Moses lived. His own mother was able to raise him and get paid to do it!

God went above and beyond to bless Jochebed for her faithfulness. Moses grew up to become one of the most influential figures in biblical history. Sometimes when we look at our situations with natural eyes, we cannot see the purpose in it. We become disabled, lose a job or a family member, and we question why it is happening to us. We don't look beyond what we can see, and we lose hope.

As a Christian, there is always a purpose for the pain. In 1 Peter 5:10, God said, "But may the God of all grace, who called us to his eternal glory by Christ Jesus, after you have suffered a while; perfect, establish strengthen and settle you." It doesn't say, "you will suffer permanent pain." This verse says, "after a while." God will restore us and strengthen us. His word will never return void.

> "So shall my word be which goes forth from my mouth; It shall not return to me void, but it shall accomplish what I please, and it shall prosper in the thing for which I sent it." Isaiah 55:11

21

Bathsheba: Victim of Circumstance
2 Samuel 11:1-5

The story of David and Bathsheba is one of the most intense narratives in the entire Bible. David was the king of Jerusalem, but he saw Bathsheba bathing one day and lusted after her. When Uriah, Bathsheba's husband, went off to battle, David sent for Bathsheba and slept with her. Bathsheba became pregnant and in order to hide his infidelity, he sent word to have Uriah stationed on the front lines. David knew this was a death sentence. After he received word of Uriah's passing, he married Bathsheba to hide his sin.

When the baby was born, God sent the prophet Nathan to confront David and inform him that his sins would not go unpunished. When David repented, God spared his life, but their baby died soon after. In time, Bathsheba learned to love David after everything he had done, and she eventually bore King Solomon.

Can you imagine how Bathsheba felt? She lost her husband, and then her child. She was put into a less than desirable situation and forced into an unexpected and difficult life. A life she never asked for.

Despite the circumstances, God had chosen Bathsheba to be part of the lineage of Jesus Christ. God saw her fit to be the ancestor of his son. She didn't know it at the time, but she had been chosen for an amazing purpose.

We don't always get to see the fruits of our labors. Sometimes the purpose of our lives is recognized after our passing. All the women in the Bible that had their stories recorded had no idea they would be influencing women for centuries to follow.

Bathsheba was a woman of strength. She endured much hardship and pain during that period of her life, but she persisted and prospered for her commitment to God.

Bathsheba trusted God despite the circumstances she found herself in, and now she is an inspiration to women all over the world. Proverbs 19:21 says, "There are many plans in a man's heart, nevertheless, the Lord's counsel will stand." It is hard to recognize hardship as part of God's plan, but that is where our faith is tested, and we grow as a Christian.

There is a quote that circulates on social media that says, "Being buried and planted look the same." I absolutely love that expression. When it looks like all hope is lost, that is when God is preparing us to grow.

> "When you pass through the waters, I will be with you; and through the rivers, they shall not overflow you. when you walk through the fire, you shall not be burned, nor shall the flame scorch you." Isaiah 43:2

22

Rachel and Leah: A Sanctioned Rivalry
Genesis 29:31-35

The story of Rachel and Leah is one of the more well-known stories in the Bible, and it begins in Genesis with Jacob. Jacob was staying with a relative named Laban. When he saw Laban's daughter Rachel, he fell in love with her. He was willing to work for Laban for seven years to earn her hand in marriage.

After the seven years were over, Laban deceived him. He gave Jacob his oldest daughter Leah instead of Rachel on their wedding night. When Jacob realized what had happened, Laban told him that he could still have Rachel, but he would have to work for another seven years.

Both sisters married to Jacob started a sibling rivalry for his affection. Leah felt unloved because she knew Rachel was the woman Jacob truly desired. Leah thought that giving Jacob heirs would make him love her more. As Leah started having children, Rachel became worried and tried to do the same for Jacob. As the story progresses, their rivalry intensified. However, in the end they fulfilled their purposes.

These two women gave Jacob 12 sons. This fulfilled the prophecy that Jacob's descendants would inherit the land of Israel. Rachel and Leah were the mothers of Israel. Their rivalry brought forth enough heirs to form the 12 Tribes.

I heard a sermon once that was titled, "You Cannot Be Called and Comfortable," the title of that sermon has resonated with me for years. If Leah was satisfied with her relationship with Jacob, she may not have pushed to have so many children. If Rachel wasn't in competition with her sister, she wouldn't have fulfilled her part of the legacy either. This rivalry had God's approval.

In the end, Leah's compassion for Rachel initiated reconciliation between the two women and they lived the rest of their lives in peace with Jacob. However, they weren't comfortable until the calling on their life was finished.

Comfort is nice. We like to be comfortable but there is no growth there. If everything is going the way we want it to, why would we push ourselves to be better? Our destinies start when we step out of our comfort zones and it's not always easy.

Comfort eventually leads to becoming stagnant. You know what else is stagnant? A swamp. John 7:38 says, "He who believe in me, as the Scripture has said, out of his heart will flow rivers of living water." Jesus is comparing a river to life. A river is constantly moving and changing. It is purified through the rocks below as it flows, and it gracefully moves around objects in its path. God doesn't want us to be like a swamp, but a river of life.

God will help us step out of that place of security we have built around ourselves. He will give us the strength we need. All we need is a little faith.

> "Fear not, for I am with you; be not dismayed, for I am your God. I will strengthen you, Yes, I will help you, I will uphold you with my righteous right hand."
> Isaiah 41:10

23

Sarah and Hagar: Mothers of Great Nations
Genesis 16:1-6

In the beginning of the Old Testament, we learn about Abraham who was a great man of God. God made a promise to Sarah and Abraham that they would conceive a son, but Sarah was growing old and impatient. She had been barren for many years, and in those days, it was customary to give your servant over to your husband to conceive a child.

Sarah decided to take matters into her own hands and send her servant Hagar to conceive a child with Abraham. When Hagar became pregnant, Sarah became jealous and angry over the situation. She beat Hagar, and Hagar fled.

Hagar was a strong woman, and she almost made it back to Egypt before an angel appeared to her. The angel told her to go back and raise her child as a Hebrew. The angel said that her son Ishmael would be special and have a great future. Pregnant and exhausted, Hagar decided to return to Sarah, but with purpose.

Fourteen years later, Sarah finally bore Abraham a son named Isaac. The rivalry between the women continued and Sarah insisted that Hagar and Ishmael be sent away. As they were walking through the desert, Ishmael began to die of thirst.

Hagar cried out to God, and he provided a spring for her to drink from. In that moment, God also made her a promise that Ishmael would father many nations. These nations became the 12 original Arabic tribes.

Genesis 16:12 says, "He shall be a wild man, his hand shall be against every man, and every man's hand against him." Ishmael was born out of defiance. Sarah did not want to wait on God and tried to do things her own way.

God kept his promises and Ishmael and Isaac both fathered great nations. However, because of Sarah's rebellion, Ishmael's descendants (Muslims) are still at war with the descendants of Judah (twelve tribes of Israel). Islam and Christianity will not live in peace until the Lord's return.

As Christians, God has forgiven us of our sins, but we are not free from the consequences of our sins. Our decisions have a lasting impact on the people around us, and our choices bleed over into other's lives.

When making a big decision, be patient and seek God's counsel first. We can do this by praying, reading our Bibles, and talking to those who have spiritual authority over us (spiritual mentors, pastors etc.).

> "Trust in the Lord with all your heart and lean not on your own understanding; in all your ways acknowledge him, and he shall direct your paths." Proverbs 3:5-6

24

Hagar: A Single Mom and a Godly Promise
Proverbs 22:6
Colossians 3:21
Ephesians 6:4

When I read over the story of Hagar, I feel compassion for her. She was an Egyptian slave sent to live in a strange land, and then told to conceive a child for the man who owned her. After becoming pregnant, she was beaten and despised by Sarah.

She ran away, but eventually returned and continued to live in strife with Sarah. After several more years, Sarah decided to send Ishmael and Hagar away for good, and she was forced to be a single mother.

Despite her situation, Hagar held on to God's promises and dedicated her life to raising her son. Her resilience made her the personification of a strong woman (Galatians 6:9).

Maybe I feel compassion for her because she was given a child by a man that left her, and she fought every day for her child's rights.

I know how hard it is to be a single mom. It takes strength, tenacity, commitment, and endurance. Essentially, you must be a warrior (Romans 8:37). There is no down time, and there is no giving up.

That child becomes everything.

Women were never meant to raise children alone. God designed the household to have a male and a female lead (Genesis 2:18-21). The statistics for children raised by a single mom are frightening. Children with absent fathers have a higher rate of delinquency, more behavioral problems, and are more likely to be living below the poverty line.

Our society has fallen away from the Biblical structure of a family, and it has prevented entire generations from reaching their full potential. The rate of homes on welfare has risen, the amount of family court proceedings has doubled, and teen suicides continue to rise. Our culture's moral compass has vanished, and we are left with shattered homes and broken children.

The greatest thing about Jesus Christ is that we can always start fresh each day. These may have been yesterday's statistics, but it doesn't have to be tomorrow's. We can make a change starting today.

We have the power to teach our children about Jesus. We have the power to bring them to church and teach them right from wrong. There are ways a single parent can raise children who contribute to society and to God's kingdom. It requires extra time and focus, but it can be done.

When we are weak, we can pull strength from the Lord, and we can do anything we put our minds to (Phil. 4:13). There is hope. We can change the dynamic of our culture by raising Godly children.

Develop your child's God-given talents by getting them involved in extracurriculars. Give them a hobby and a goal to work for to keep them focused in the right direction. Having a group of like-minded and positive friends, will help them stay strong when peer pressure starts to weigh on them.

> "Have I not commanded you? Be strong and of
> good courage; do not be afraid, nor be dismayed, for

the Lord your God is with you wherever you go."
Joshua 1:9

Reference:

1. https://www.ncjrs.gov/App/publications/Abstract.aspx?id=167327

25

Sarah: Required Patience
Genesis 17:18-21

I want to make sure that I do not completely villainize Sarah through this Bible study. Sarah was chosen to be the mother of many powerful nations. Her descendants consisted of several kings and eventually Jesus Christ. Jesus's lineage begins with Sarah and Abraham.

Sarah was nearly 90 years old when she finally gave birth to Isaac. God had given Abraham the promise of a son over 15 years prior. Eventually her faith did waiver, and she decided to make her own heir through Hagar, but can we blame her?

I know it would be very hard for me to hold on to a promise God had made that long ago. I would question myself, and I would question whether I understood the promise right. A lot of us would.

When Hagar finally became pregnant, the Bible says she started to despise Sarah (Genesis 16:4). The animosity went both ways. More than likely, Hagar's bitterness increased during that time because of hormones, but it could have been intentional arrogance as well. Between Sarah's jealousy and Hagar's antagonizing, Sarah lashed out on her.

Regardless of Sarah's actions, an angel appeared before Abraham and let him know that his heir was not to be Ishmael, but Isaac. Nothing she had done had stopped God's word from being accomplished.

Do you ever struggle with trusting God? When we read the Bible, we see miracles accomplished, but sometimes it is hard to believe anything like that could happen to us. Our focus needs to be on being the exception. Sarah was the exception.

I have a brain tumor. It is not cancerous right now and has not grown in several years. Some people may get depressed and see that as a death sentence, but there is no reason why I can't be the exception. I have heard of tumors disappearing and that is where my focus lies. God's will for each of our lives may vary, but one thing that is constant, it is God's will for all of us to be healed.

God always fulfills his promises. Even in our imperfections, God will always keep his word (Joshua 21:45). We cannot prevent God from achieving his will for our lives. Rest in the knowledge that God wants what is best for us and that our inadequacies will not stop him from taking care of us. God will always take care of his children.

> "Therefore say to them, 'Thus says the Lord God: none of my words will be postponed any more, but the word which I speak will be done,' says the Lord God." Ezekiel 12:28

26

Mary, Mother of Jesus and Elisabeth: Get Connected
Luke 1:32-37

Elisabeth was the mother of John the Baptist. She was also a cousin of Mary, the mother of Jesus. When Mary heard that Elisabeth was pregnant, she went to visit her. Mary spoke to Elisabeth when she arrived and upon hearing her voice, John jumped in Elisabeth's womb. At that moment, Elisabeth was filled with the Holy Spirit, and she blessed Mary.

I don't believe it was a coincidence that Mary and Elisabeth were part of the same family. God knew they were both going to need strong familial support to get through their pregnancies.

I can only imagine the emotional stress Mary felt as an unwed mother, and the physical stress Elisabeth felt as an older woman, carrying a child. They needed each other. Hebrews 10:24 says, "And let us consider one another in order to stir up love and good works."

God did not make us to live this life alone. We all need someone we can depend on. Society today wants us to believe that needing each other is a sign of weakness.

Divine Positioning for a Powerful Purpose

However, the Bible is very clear that we are here to bear one another's burdens (Galatians 6:2). There is nothing wrong with needing help. From the very beginning, interdependence was God's will for us, not independence.

In a social media laden world, it is easy to put off outings with friends, or even going to church on Sundays. We know we can just connect through our laptops, but that doesn't allow for face to face interaction. Community is important to our well-being.

Inspiration is imperative for motivation. We become inspired by connecting to others and hearing their stories. When we have people cheering us on and supporting us, we gain the determination needed to keep going.

It also keeps us accountable. When we are surrounded with like-minded believers, we can reach out for counsel and prayer to strengthen us through our trials. This is why finding a good church is necessary to Christian growth. Find a group of people who are there to encourage you, pray for you, and get connected.

> "As iron sharpens iron, so a man sharpens the countenance of his friend." Proverbs 27:17

27

Ruth: Fruits of the Spirit
Proverbs 31:10-31
Galatians 5:22-25

Ruth is the perfect example of a Proverbs 31 woman. When Ruth's husband died, she stayed with her mother-in-law Naomi, who was also a widow. She went to Judah with Naomi and cared for her. It would have been perfectly acceptable for Ruth to return to her homeland and find another husband there, but she stayed.

Her loyalty to Naomi was a beautiful thing and God blessed her for it. As she was working hard to collect food for herself and Naomi each day, she caught the eye of Boaz. Boaz was a good man and wealthy man. He married Ruth, and their marriage has been used as a model of a true Biblical relationship for generations.

Ruth embodied the fruits of the spirit. The fruits of the spirit are the result of using the gifts of the spirit (the way God intended). These are: love, joy, peace, kindness, gentleness, goodness, faithfulness, gentleness, and self -control (Galatians 5:22-23). When you start to use your God given gifts, you begin to possess these qualities effortlessly.

Divine Positioning for a Powerful Purpose

Most of us have seen the requirements of a Proverbs 31 woman and have become overwhelmed with the level of perfection attained in that chapter. However, while we should strive to be the best version of ourselves, we should not become frustrated where we fall short. It is necessary that we are kind to ourselves and understand we are doing the best we can.

When we try to reach a level of unattainable perfection by running ourselves in to the ground; we become angry, tense, and stressed. That is not what God wants for us.

Instead of focusing on perfection, we need to focus on our purpose. As we are working on our purpose, we will start to see a natural shift in our mindset. When we start to develop peace, anxiety goes away. When we develop love, anger disappears. When we start to develop kindness, animosity vanishes. Ephesians 5:8 says, "For you were once darkness, but now you are light in the Lord. Walk as children of light."

As we grow in Christ, the negative aspects of our selves fade away. That darkness is no longer who we are. Today, I urge you to shift your perspective to be more like Ruth. Focus more on your spiritual gifts and you will naturally become the virtuous woman in Proverbs 31.

"This is the message which we have heard from Him and declare to you, that God is light and in Him is no darkness at all." 1 John 1:5

28

Anna: A Servant's Heart
Luke 2:36-38

During Jesus' childhood, we learn about a prophetess named Anna. There are only a few women who were regarded to hold such an esteemed position. Deborah, Miriam, and Isaiah's wife were among the others. To be held at this level of importance speaks of Anna's dedication.

When Anna's husband died, she devoted her time to serving God. She was found in the temple day and night worshipping God. Her commitment to God was rewarded when she had the opportunity to see Baby Jesus in the temple. She was among the first people to observe the Savior of our world.

Anna embodied the personification of Jesus Christ himself. God came to Earth as a servant. He didn't come to control and dominate us, but to love and help us. Jesus even submitted himself to death at the cross (Phil. 2:8). He died for us.

Not only are we required to possess a servant's heart, but we are expected to have the right motivation as well. Are we only helping to be praised? Or are we serving to be like Jesus? Mark 10:45 says, "For even the Son of Man did not come to be served but to serve, and to give his life a ransom for many."

Divine Positioning for a Powerful Purpose

Our society is very self-focused. It is centered around satisfying our own needs and personal happiness. While happiness and perfect peace are the goal, we are striving to achieve it by worldly means. We filter our entire lives through social media and forget about the state of our souls. We become busy with fixing our physical imperfections and aren't concerned with the condition of our hearts.

God will give us the desires of our hearts and a joy that is only found in Him. However, we must obtain it through Christ. Our goals of happiness are not wrong, but how we are trying to access them are. If we focus on serving one another and fulfilling our purpose, these gifts will come effortlessly. We won't have to work for peace and happiness. It will naturally become a state of mind.

As Christians, we should be looking for opportunities to help others. There is joy found in selflessness. We don't have to help someone every day, but we should be willing. God is looking for that willingness to serve. Let him know that he can place someone in your path to serve, just as Christ did for us.

> "Let each of you look out not only for his own interests, but also for the interests of others... And being found in the appearance of man, he humbled himself and became obedient to the point of death, even the death of the cross." Philippians 2:4,8

29

Joanna: Fighting Social Stigmas
Luke 8:1-3

Joanna was a prominent member of King Herod's court. She was the wife of Cuza, who oversaw Herod's estates. After King Herod had John the Baptist beheaded, Joanna was healed by Jesus. The Bible doesn't state whether the two events were connected, but I believe she was disgusted by the beheading and sought out Jesus.

Joanna could have led a comfortable life. She had riches and every luxury afforded to them at the time, because of her societal position. However, she knew she was missing something.

There is something inside of us that cannot be fulfilled with the treasures and comforts of the world. Our souls desire to be connected to God and we feel that emptiness until we fill that void with Jesus (Psalm 42:2) (Colossians 2:10).

Joanna recognized the need for something more and left her life of extravagance to follow Jesus. Can you imagine the social stigma she would have faced? It was considered shameful for an unmarried woman to follow around a group of men. Can you imagine how much more disapproval she felt from her community as a married woman? I can only assume her husband suffered ridicule for her actions as well, but she didn't care what society had to say about her. She knew that Jesus was the son of God, and she was rewarded by having the opportunity to be present at Jesus resurrection.

How many times in life have we let the opinions of others stop us from doing what we know is right? When we put ourselves out there, we become vulnerable and that's scary.

There have been moments I felt that God was leading me to post something, but because I didn't have any "likes" after a few hours, I took it down. I let my insecurities get in the way. It may seem small, but someone needed to see that post. Since I had decided to take it down, they may not have received the encouragement they needed that day.

We cannot inspire others without becoming vulnerable ourselves. People need to hear our stories. They need to know they are not alone. It's hard to expose our lives because we are opening ourselves up to criticism from a harsh world, but God can't work with someone who is shut down.

Vulnerability leaves us unguarded, but God has promised his protection (Proverbs 18:10). The first time I wrote a blog post and shared it, I was terrified. My heart was racing, and I checked the comments every few minutes. Over time, it eventually became easier for me to share my story and the goodness of God in a public forum.

The fear of what people though dissipated, and I gained confidence. I allowed God to work through me, and he has healed my entire life through the process.

Become vulnerable, use your gifts, inspire others, and let God position you for purpose.

> "Then Jesus said to his disciples, 'If anyone desires to come after me, let him deny himself and take up his cross and follow me.'" Matthew 16:24

30

Tabitha: A Kind Heart
Acts 9:36-42

In the Bible, Tabitha is regarded as a good woman, whom everybody loved. She was known by her heart and her deeds (Acts 9:36). The writer of Acts doesn't mention her place in society; whether she was rich or had a husband. She was known for her character (Matthew 7:16). Tabitha had a heart after God's own.

When Tabitha died, the entire community was affected. Two men were sent to get Peter and bring him back to her. After Peter arrived, he got on his knees to pray and said, "Tabitha arise." She opened her eyes, and Peter helped her stand.

The Bible says, "Many believed" after she was risen from the dead (Acts 9:42). Tabitha's heart was in the right place. She knew her purpose in this world and fulfilled it daily through her community. People loved and respected her for her kindness.

She was specifically chosen to be brought back from the dead because of the respect people had for her, and for her devotion to God. The Lord knew how great her testimony would be because of who she was.

Our hearts are formed in the womb before our brains, and they contain their own Central Nervous System. Basically, our hearts send a lot more signals to the brain, than the brain send to the heart. Until recently, I never understood the significance of this. Everything (life) begins with the state of our hearts. Whatever we are feeling in our hearts, is what is transmitted to our brains.

Working on our minds is important, but the state of our hearts will be reflected in our thoughts, feelings, and emotions. Proverbs 4:23 says, "Above all else, guard your heart, for everything you do flows from it." It all starts right there.

We can transform the condition of our hearts by focusing on gratitude. We can take a walk outside and thank God for a beautiful day, or help an elderly couple clean their home. When we start to live a life of kindness and appreciation, the shape of our hearts will change.

Light and dark cannot occupy the same space. The more we focus on the positive (light), the less room there is for the negative (dark). Let's concentrate on the good things (Phil. 4:8) and see how much more God is able to use us.

> "For all things are for your sakes, that grace, having
> spread through the many, may cause thanksgiving to
> abound to the glory of God."
> 2 Corinthians 4:15

31

Even the Chosen Fall:
A Common Theme
Romans 3:23
1 Corinthians 1:27
John 15:16

As I read over the accounts of Martha, Rachel, Leah, Eve, and several other amazing Biblical women, I noticed a similar element among their stories. They all fell at one point in their walk with God. Martha became bitter, Miriam became jealous, Sarah became impatient, and Hagar and Eve had moments of rebellion, but these women always found their way back to God.

When we become Christians, we profess our faith to the Lord Jesus Christ and make a commitment to follow the Word of God to the best of our ability every day.

As we grow in Christ, we grow as a person. We become more patient, we develop strength and resilience, and we tend to feel a general sense of fulfillment.

However, over time, we can become negligent if we do not remain vigilant. We can develop bad habits without even realizing it. Maybe we get annoyed with a new coworker and foster a breeding ground for gossip in the workplace. Maybe we start skimping on tithes because of some unexpected monetary circumstances. What seems like a harmless event leaves the door open for it to grow into a bad habit. Those bad habits will snowball into multiple poor life decisions.

It happens to all of us. However, it doesn't mean that God has taken his hand off us. We are still his children. 2 Corinthians 1:21-22 says, "Now he who establishes us with you in Christ and anointed us in God, who also sealed us and gave us the Holy Spirit in our hearts as a pledge."

When we make a profession of faith, God seals us and gives us the Holy Spirit to guide us through life. To *seal* is, "to secure definitively." Our place by his side in heaven is secured even if we make mistakes, as long as we are still attempting to grow as Christians.

We are imperfect, God knows that and doesn't expect perfection, but He does expect us to strive for perfection. The Holy Spirit will start to convict you when you're heading in the wrong direction. He will gently nudge you back to the way you should go.

Conviction is a gift from God. It shouldn't be seen as a source of punishment. God only wants what is best for us and that still small voice is how he guides us towards correcting our paths.

Recently, I was rude to a woman who works the front desk at my children's school. I was having a rough week, and she happened to be the woman at the desk both times I went in there with a bad attitude. God convicted me, and I chose to rectify the situation. I am sure she deals with grumpy parents all the time but if we ever meet again, I want her to see me as a Christian, not as the scary mom at the school.

I bought her a candle and apologized. I told her I could only imagine how difficult her job was keeping track of so many children every day and she was doing a great job. I can tell she wasn't expecting something like that. I also saw the smile on her face through the glass as I walked back to my car. From now on, I will be much more aware of my attitude when I enter the school.

This is how we break cycles that will be damaging to our walk with Christ. We recognize the Holy Spirit's prodding of our heart and do what we can to fix the situation. By changing how we operate, we change how people see us. This is how we will also change the world's view of Christianity.

It all starts with the little things.

"Now I rejoice, not that you were made sorry, but that your sorrow led to repentance. For you were made sorry in a godly manner, that you might suffer loss from us in nothing. For godly sorrow produces repentance leading to salvation, not to be regretted; but the sorrow of the world produces death." 2 Corinthians 7:9-10

32

The Maid from Israel: A Little Girl's Integrity
2 Kings 5:1-4

During a Syrian raid on Israel, a young girl was taken captive. This young girl was sent to be a servant to Naaman, the field commander of the Syrian army. Naaman was a unique case. He had leprosy. Most people with leprosy were sent beyond the walls and ostracized. However, because of his prominence in the army, he was able to remain as head of his household.

The Bible does not say how long it took the little girl to gain the trust of Naaman, but she eventually approached his wife and told her of Elisha. Elisha was an Old Testament prophet and healer living in Samaria. The little girl believed he could heal Naaman. Trusting that the she was telling the truth, the king of Damascus allowed Naaman to go to Israel in search of the prophet. Naaman was going into the land of his enemies in search of their help!

In order to show Naaman that only the God of Israel can truly heal, Elisha refused to see him. Instead, Elisha told Naaman to take seven baths in the Jordan river and then he would be clean. Naaman was angry, but eventually agreed to do what the prophet said, and he was healed. The commander of the Syrian army had been healed by the God of Israel!

In 2 Kings 5:15 and 17, Naaman returned to Elisha. He said to the prophet, "Indeed, now I know that there is no God in all the earth, except in Israel... For your servant will no longer offer either burnt offering or sacrifice to other gods, but to the Lord."

Even though this young girl was taken from her home and forced to be a servant, she remained faithful to God and earned the trust of Naaman and his wife. The integrity and bravery of this young girl changed the life of a very prominent Syrian commander.

The Little Maid from Israel held strong to her faith. She remained honest and trustworthy despite her situation. She had integrity.

When we are in the middle of hardship, the Bible tells us to rejoice always and give thanks in everything (I Thessalonians 5:16 and 18). It can be hard to see the good in a bad situation, but we can rest in knowing that all things work together for good to them who love God (Romans 8:28).

Don't let circumstances affect your integrity. God gives responsibility to those he knows he can trust. If you want God to use you, show him he can trust you. Draw near to God and he will draw near to you (James 4:8).

> "My brethren, count it all joy when you fall into various trials. Knowing that the testing of your faith produces patience." James 1:2-3

33

Priscilla: Prominence in the First Church
Acts 18:24-26

Priscilla and her husband Aquila were tent makers. They resided in Corinth after fleeing the persecution of the Jewish people in Italy. They became great friends of Paul and helped him establish the Corinthian church.

When Paul left for Ephesus, Priscilla and Aquila went with him. They established another church in Ephesus, and Paul entrusted them with the congregation when he departed for Syria (Acts 18:18-21).

When Priscilla and Aquila heard Apollos preaching the Gospel, they noticed that his preaching was incomplete. The Bible describes Apollos as an eloquent man, that is competent in Scripture (Acts 18:24) but he needed a little more direction on the significance of the resurrection. Priscilla and Aquila pulled him aside and explained the Gospel to him more accurately, and Apollos accepted their instruction.

As we look at historical landmarks in Rome, we can see that Priscilla's influence reached a significant amount of people. One of the oldest Catacombs in Rome is named after her, as well as a church. In a society where women were rarely put in positions of power, Priscilla had gained the respect of the people.

I think it is important to note that Priscilla is never mentioned without her husband Aquila. While she may have had more influence over the community, her husband was always there to support her. They worked together, traveled together, instructed Apollos together, and grew two successful congregations together. Their marriage always placed God first, and they were successful because of it.

These two did not shy away from hard work. They traveled to a foreign land and started a new church on two separate occasions. Priscilla and Aquila were also brave. In Romans 16:4, Paul states that they risked their lives for him.

While Priscilla and Aquila may have been great on their own, they were even stronger together. God's intention for marriage is for us to complement one another. We are to encourage each other and grow together. Putting God at the center of our relationships and seeking him first will lead to a fruitful and successful relationship.

Aquila loved his wife and supported her even when she outshined him. Priscilla allowed Aquila to be the head of the household and she followed his direction. Together they trusted God to guide them and respected his design for marriage.

What can we do to establish Christ in our relationships? How can we include him daily to improve our marriages? Our relationship with God will reflect in our relationship with our significant other. Start taking time out each day to focus on God first and see how your relationship strengthens along with your spiritual life.

> "Two are better than one because they have a good reward for their labor. For if they fall, one will lift up his companion." Ecclesiastes 4:9-10

References:

1. https://honorsaharchive.blogspot.com/2008/07/early-christian-imagery-in-catacombs-of.html
2. https://scotscollege.org/stations-churches-of-rome-saint-prisca/

34

Woman at the Well: The Beginning of Evangelism
John 4:7-15

The Woman at the Well lived in Samaria. She went to the well in the middle of the day to avoid the other women. Drawing water from the well was a time when the women would socialize with one another in the cool of the morning, or in the shade of the evening.

The fact that she went during the hottest point of the day shows that her people did not accept her. She was an outcast. This Samarian woman had had five husbands and was living with a sixth man unmarried. She was the subject of much gossip and public scrutiny.

One day when she was at the well, Jesus approached her and asked for a drink. She was surprised and said, "How is it that you, a Jew, ask a drink from me, a Samaritan woman?" In that time, Jews and Samaritans did not have anything to do with each other. Jesus answered and said, "If you knew the gift of God, and who it is says to you, 'Give me a drink,' you would have asked him and he would have given you living water." (John 4:9-10)

Jesus told her that whoever drank from the well would thirst again.

But whoever drank of the living water, would never thirst again. The Woman at the Well was thirsty, but not in the traditional sense. She was craving more from life. She wanted hope and a purpose. She asked Jesus to give her the living water.

When the disciples returned to Jesus, they were shocked to see him conversing alone with a woman. As the woman listened to Jesus, she was changed. She felt complete and had hope for the first time. She left her water pot and went to tell the city about Jesus.

This woman was not liked by her people. In order for them to listen her, they would have had to notice something different about her; something that couldn't be explained. After hearing her testimony, the people flocked to Jesus, and Jesus stayed with them for two days.

We all reach a point in our lives where we feel like we are just going through the motions. We have no drive, no hope, and no desire to do much of anything. We let depression set in and, we lose sight of our reason for being here. We forget that we were created uniquely by the God of the universe for a specific purpose.

This woman realized that the answer to her sorrow was right in front of her. All she had to do was reach out and accept the gift of eternal life that Jesus was offering her.

Her past didn't matter. She was forgiven of her sins and felt a level of peace that can only be experienced through Christ. She was so excited about her encounter that she wanted to share it with everyone around her. These were the same people that gossiped about her and treated her poorly. She forgave them and invited them to hear the Gospel.

The Woman at the Well is a perfect example of the type of Christians we should be. Have you ever avoided talking to someone about Christ because they were mean to you? Or maybe you were afraid they would laugh at you? Jesus said to go into all the world and preach the Gospel (Mark 16:15). He didn't tell us to only speak to certain groups of people. He said, "All the world."

This woman was the first evangelist in history. God chose a woman to become the first evangelist!

When I studied this Samarian woman, I didn't realize how

inspirational she was going to be to me. However, anyone who can forgive their enemies and want them to experience the love of Jesus without a second thought is a true role model for all women.

"Whoever drinks of this water will thirst again, but whoever drinks of the water that I shall give him will never thirst. But the water that I shall give him will become in him a fountain of water springing up into everlasting life." John 4:13-14

35

Mary Magdalene: From Unrefined to Sanctified
John 20:11-18

Mary Magdalene came from a fishing village called Magdala. When Jesus was passing through her town, he healed her from seven evil spirits. From that moment on, Mary followed Jesus and became a devoted follower and disciple.

Luke 8:3 states that she was one of the women who were funding Jesus's ministry, which indicates she may have been very wealthy. Mary was one of the few that followed Jesus to the cross even when his other disciples had not. She waited until he was taken down from the cross and went with him to his grave. Her faith in Jesus was undeniable.

Mary was also the first person to notice that the stone had been rolled away from his tomb when Jesus rose from the grave on the third day. In shock, she brought Peter and John back to the grave to show them that he was no longer in the tomb. Peter and John had no explanation for what had happened, but acknowledged that she was right. They returned home, but Mary stayed to continue mourning.

A little while later, she looked up and saw two angels sitting in

Jesus tomb. They said, "Woman, why are you weeping?" She responded and said, "Because they have taken away my Lord and I do not know where they have laid him." (John 20:13-14)

In that moment, Jesus stood in front of her. She did not recognize him and assumed he was the gardener. She asked him if he had moved the body of Jesus Christ and if she could retrieve it, but Jesus looked down at her and said, "Mary!"

When she realized it was Jesus standing in front of her, she jumped up and embraced him. He told her not to cling to him because he had not ascended yet, but to go tell the others of the things he had spoken to her.

Because of her dedication to Jesus, she was the first one to witness the resurrection, and the first person Jesus spoke to after being raised from the grave. What an honor to be present at one of the most important moments in history!

I believe that the prominence of women in these Biblical accounts is intentional. God created women to be companions and helpmates to man, but he wanted to make sure the importance of women was not diminished. We were made to complete man, but with our own strengths and purposes.

Jesus went against the culture of his time and spent a significant time talking to and teaching women. He didn't practice chauvinism, which was common in this period of Biblical history.

Jesus has always seen the uniqueness and beauty in each one of us. God created the entire universe and felt that we were a necessary part of that design. Everything he does is deliberate and purposeful for those of us that are saved to give us hope and a future (Jeremiah 29:11).

Think of the majesty of the mountains, the violence of the ocean waves, the simplicity of a flower blooming, and the pure joy of a small puppy. This world is an amazing place! While we immerse ourselves in awe of God's creation, we need to be able to look in the mirror and feel the same way about how God created us.

> "I will praise you for I am fearfully and wonderfully made. Marvelous are your works and that my soul knows very well." Psalms 139:14

36

Abigail: A Calm Disposition
1 Samuel 25:24-33

In the Bible, Abigail is said to be an attractive and intelligent woman (1 Samuel 25:3). She was the wife of a cruel and bitter man named Nabal. When David was running from Saul, he tried to seek shelter with them.

Nabal was a wealthy man and had more than enough provisions to spare for David and his men. David had been kind to Nabal's shepherds in the past, and this request for shelter was not unreasonable.

In 1 Samuel 25:10-11, Nabal refused David's request saying, "Who is this David? Shall I then take my bread, my water, and my meat that I have killed for my shearers and give it to men when I do not know where they are from?" This response infuriated David, and he swore to kill every man connected to Nabal's household.

When Abigail heard of David's plan to destroy her home, she packed two hundred loaves of bread, two wine skins, five sheep, five seahs of roasted grain, one hundred clusters of raisins, and two hundred fig cakes. She loaded these provisions onto donkeys and set out to meet David on the road in an attempt to change his mind (1 Samuel 25:18).

Abigail was a very brave woman. She was riding out in secret to meet four hundred angry men on their way to seek vengeance on her home! She was going to apologize for Nabal's behavior and ask David to show mercy.

When she reached David's men, she threw herself on the ground in front of David and pleaded for her husband's life saying, "Please, let not my lord regard this scoundrel Nabal. For as his name is, so is he. Nabal is his name and folly is with him (1 Samuel 25:25)." Abigail showed David that she knew what kind of man Nabal really is, but asks David to reconsider anyway.

David agrees to spare her household and thanks her for stopping him from killing those men (1 Samuel 25:33). He sees her as a blessing from God and sent her home in peace (1 Samuel 25:35).

When Abigail approached David, she treated him with respect. At the time, David was no more than an outlaw while her household was one of wealth and economic status. However, she calmly pleaded her cause with reverence. Abigail understood that a gentle word was the best way to be diplomatic.

Have you ever been in a situation where you lashed out at someone and they reciprocated in the same manner? Both parties end up becoming defensive and angry; nothing gets accomplished except hurt feelings. When we can respond with kindness and use our words to communicate in a calm manner, we will almost always see better results.

In Proverbs 16:24, the Bible says, "Pleasant words are like a honeycomb. Sweetness to the soul and health to the bones." If Abigail had charged at David and yelled at him, she would have been met with the same hostility. She showed him admiration and the love of God through her actions. Romans 12 is a great chapter on brotherly love and how we should act towards each other. Verse 21 says, "Do not be overcome by evil, but overcome evil with good."

When we step back and look at people who lash out in anger, they're usually hurt. Hurt people try to cause pain to others. David was hurt by Nabal's actions towards his men, and Abigail's response diffused the situation. She showed David he was worthy of the respect her husband lacked. Nabal became ill and died shortly after Abigail returned home. Abigail's integrity was rewarded when David asked her to be his wife once he heard of Nabal's passing. She became the wife of a future king. We can show this same attitude towards others who are hurt. We can show everyone that they are worthy of love and treat them with kindness despite how they act towards us. We do not have to keep toxic people around, but we can treat them how Jesus would.

"Repay no one evil for evil. Have regard for good things in the sight of all men. If it is possible, as much as depends on you, live peaceably with all men." Romans 12:17-18

37

Hannah: Unwavering Dedication
1 Samuel 2:1-10

Hannah was the barren wife of Elkahan. Elkahan's other wife Peninnah was able to have children and she had no problem reminding Hannah of her inability to conceive. Hannah received a double portion from their husband as well (1 Samuel 1:5). This implies that she was loved more even though she was barren, and I think this contributed to Peninnah's taunting. She was jealous of Elkahan's affection for Hannah.

Hannah became desperate and stopped eating. Her husband was sad because he didn't understand why she was so upset (1 Samuel 1:8). Hannah went to the tabernacle to pray and wept in anguish (1 Samuel 1:10). She vowed to give her son back to God as a Nazarite if he would bless her with a child. The vow of a Nazarite was a voluntary commitment made by young men who wanted to dedicate their lives to the service of the Lord. However, Hannah made this vow for her unborn child (Numbers 6:1-8).

When the priest at the tabernacle saw her crying out, he accused her of being drunk. She told him that she was not drunk but pouring her soul out to God. The priest answered and said, "Go in peace, and the God of Israel will grant your petition which you have asked of him (1 Samuel 1:15 and 17)." Hannah left the tabernacle that day with renewed faith.

Shortly after, Hannah conceived a son. She named him Samuel and as soon as he was weaned, she brought him back to the Lord's house where he stayed indefinitely. Every year Hannah would make him a new robe and bring it to him when they gave their yearly sacrifice (1 Samuel 2:19).

Samuel grew up to be a prophet and a judge. He also had a significant influence on King Saul and King David. Hannah was also blessed with four more children after Samuel.

Hannah wanted a child so bad that she went to God and prayed relentlessly. She prayed so hard that the priest accused her of being drunk! She was determined to reach God and stayed as long as it took to get her breakthrough. Her persistence paid off and she was granted a child. A child that had great influence over kings.

When we are reaching out to God for a breakthrough, it requires dedication. Maybe the reason Hannah had stopped eating before she went to pray was to fast. Jesus taught many years later in the New Testament that some breakthroughs required both prayer and fasting.

Reaching God in this manner also requires patience, faith and forgiveness. Hannah had to forgive Peninnah before she could receive her blessing. She would not have been granted a child if she did not first forgive her rival for being so cruel to her. We cannot have hatred or spite in our hearts when we are fervently seeking God to bless our lives (Ephesians 4:26-27).

When we reach a point of desperation that only God can fix, we must be persistent and pray that God will align our lives with his will. How do we know that what we are praying for is God's will for us? If we are praying for healing, we can be reassured that it is God's will for us to be whole (Isaiah 53:5). If we are praying for peace of mind, God will deliver us from mental torment as well (Psalm 34:18).

God doesn't always answer prayers in the manner we assume. Some answers require patience. God's timing is very different from our own. When we are focused and determined in our prayer, we can be confident that whatever the outcome, it will be the absolute best solution. Jeremiah 29:11 says, "For I know the thoughts I think towards you says the Lord. Thoughts of peace and not of evil. To give you a future and a hope."

God won't leave you in your mess. He will help you out of whatever situation you find yourself in.

> "Then you will call upon me and go and pray to me and I will listen to you. And you will seek me and find me when you search for me with your whole heart. I will be found by you, says the Lord, and I will bring you back from your captivity." Jeremiah 29:12-14

38

Rizpah: A Tenacious Vigil
2 Samuel 21:10-14

In the Old Testament, Rizpah was one of Saul's concubines. Much like Bathsheba, she became a victim of circumstance through the violence of war. When Saul came into a place of power, he broke a covenant made by Joshua with the Gibeonites. This covenant was sealed by the Lord that they would not destroy the Gibeonites by the sword. Despite this oath, Saul decided to abolish the enemies of Israel through war.

A famine took over the land for three years, and God told David it was a result of Saul's annihilation of the Gibeonites. They demanded that Saul's sons be hanged for what he had done, and David complied. Seven innocent children were killed through their thirst for revenge, and two of those children were Rizpah's.

The law stated that anyone who was hanged be buried by the end of that first day. However, the bitterness of the Gibeonites over Saul's actions was shown through their lack of respect for the law and care for the dead. They allowed Saul's children to hang until there was nothing left.

For weeks, Rizpah spread sackcloth on a rock and watched over the bodies of these innocent children. She protected them from the vultures and wild animals.

Rizpah's tenacity eventually gained the attention of David. When he heard about what she had done, he remembered that Jonathan and Saul's bones were still laying in the street. David commanded that Saul's bones, and the bones of the sons Rizpah had watched over, be buried in the family tomb together (2 Samuel 21:14). When David did this, the famine was lifted.

Rizpah remained committed to her cause until God showed mercy and stopped the famine (2 Samuel 21:10). Sometimes we get in situations where we must make a choice. We can either follow the majority, or stand for what we believe is right. As Christians we should be an example of Christ. People should be able to set us apart as followers of Jesus by our actions.

In Galatians 6:9, the Bible says, "And let us not grow weary in doing good. For in due season, we shall reap if we do not lose heart." Rizpah's determination is a perfect example of this verse. She did the right thing despite the possibility of public scrutiny and brought honor back to Saul's household.

Making the right choice is not always an easy task but God commands us to stand firm (Ephesians 6:11). We can draw on the strength we receive from the Lord and trust that he will have our back in whatever situations arise. Our time on this earth is short. What kind of imprint will you leave behind?

"Therefore my beloved brethren, be steadfast, immovable, always abounding in the work of the Lord. Knowing that your labor is not in vain in the Lord." 1 Corinthians 15:58

39

Lydia: An Unexpected Encounter
Acts 16:11-15

Lydia is first seen in the New Testament when Paul visits Macedonia. Lydia was a seller of purple cloth. More than likely she was a wealthy woman since purple was expensive and a color of royalty. Lydia was a believer in God, but she wasn't a Christian. When she heard the gospel preached, God opened her heart, and she was baptized along with her entire household (Acts 16:14).

When God opened her heart to hear the gospel, she immediately became a servant of Jesus Christ. She invited Paul and his travel companions to stay in her home. Her hospitality was evident of the work God was doing in her spirit.

Paul returned to Macedonia some time later in his ministry, and he met with other believers in Lydia's home. This leads us to believe that she had stayed active in the church and was closely associated with other Christians (Acts 16:40).

When Paul found Lydia, she was sitting by the river's edge with a group of women honoring the Sabbath. Paul's visit was not expected, and Lydia's life was forever changed in that moment.

Most of us can remember the time we were saved. Some of us were in church but a lot of us were not. One thing I believe we can agree on is that our salvation was not expected. We don't always understand how God works or why he works the way he does but as Christians we should always be prepared to be the vessel in which God uses to save someone else.

The moment we are saved, we are changed. There is something noticeably different about us, and there is a light that shines from within us (John 8:12). The emptiness and longing we felt disappears and we are made whole. No one even liked The Woman at The Well, but they listened because they saw something different in her. They saw something they wanted.

Do you emanate God's love in your daily walk? If God put someone in your path for salvation, would your character draw them in or deter them from pressing forward?

As Christians, we understand what it is like to have the comfort of a loving Father in heaven but before we were saved, most of us were hesitant to believe a God we can't see could really be what we needed. We surrendered to God's love because the people sharing his love made us feel secure and safe.

Would you have been receptive to someone who complained on social media all the time? Would you have listened to someone who didn't show the best character behind closed doors? Would you have been apt to believe a person who never follows through with their word? People are watching us and in our "share all" society, it is even more important that we are mindful of our behavior.

Lydia immediately welcomed Paul into her home and continued following Jesus when he left. Her character didn't waiver because Paul left. God can't use us to bring others to Christ if we are not living the life we are supposed to live, consistently.

On judgement day, we will answer for those that were led astray by our actions (Ezekiel 33:8). When you are standing in front of God, how will your report look?

Divine Positioning for a Powerful Purpose

"But I say to you that every idle word men may speak, they will give account of it in the day of judgement. For by your words you will be justified, and by your words you will be condemned." Matthew 12:36-37

40

Phebe: An Important Position
Romans 16:1-2
Titus 2:7-8

Phebe is mentioned in the New Testament when Paul introduces her in the beginning of Romans chapter 16. He states that Phebe is a servant of the church. Some translations use the word deaconess to show her prominence in the church.

Whether she was a simple servant of the Lord or held in an esteemed position of authority is irrelevant. She was trusted by Paul to be his letter carrier. Her reliable character may be the only reason we have certain parts of the book of Romans today.

Paul did not care that Phebe was a woman, he only wanted the best person for the job regardless of gender. It was her character that gained her respect and authority in the church.

I believe Phebe was also strong, brave, and had unwavering faith. Traveling as a single woman in those days was dangerous, but she trusted God to protect her on her journey. She didn't allow fear or doubt to hinder her from her calling.

When you think of someone who has good character, who comes

to mind? Is it someone who is honest and kind? Or maybe someone who is compassionate and giving? Christian character comes from the indwelling of the Holy Spirit. When we are saved, God changes our hearts (Ezekiel 36:2) and gives us the Holy Spirit to guide us (Romans 5:5).

We make the choice to follow Christ and develop good character. In turn, our character will start to affect our decisions. The old self may have been cold and heartless, but the new self, responds with love.

Developing Godly character is the act of fostering the actual character of God. At his core, God is pure love and there are several ways we can strengthen that character in our own lives.

We can guard our thoughts (Proverbs 23:7), protect our hearts (Proverbs 4:23), study God's Word (Psalm 119:105), give to others ((Luke 6:35), practice gratitude (1 Thessalonians 5:18), forgive one another (Colossians 3:13), fellowship with other believers (James 5:16), and just enjoy life (Psalm 118:24).

Let go of past pain and regret, and choose today to be more Christ-like. We cannot move forward if we are looking backwards. When Jesus died on the cross for our sins, it was with the intention that we could be saved and have a fresh start in life. All that is required is to accept him as our Savior.

How amazing is it that we serve a God that died for us? Every religion has a god that demands a sacrifice. We serve the only God that became a sacrifice.

Accept the gift of a new life today and become the person God intended you to be. Develop Godly character and as you change your own life, you will change the lives of those around you simultaneously.

It is impossible to hide the light of God in our lives when we are saved. We can use that light to illuminate the lives of others and share it with them if they are willing to receive it.

Phebe's character preceded her on her journey to Rome because she had allowed God to change her life. She followed God's laws and worked hard to develop her character through Christ. She influenced a lot of people including Paul! You never know who you will influence or what opportunities will arise when you are living the way God intended.

Sheena Holbrooks

"But also for this very reason, giving all diligence, add to your faith virtue, to virtue knowledge, to knowledge self-control, to self-control perseverance, to perseverance godliness, to godliness brotherly kindness, and to brotherly kindness love." 2 Peter 1:5-7

41

Orpah: Taking the Easy Way
Ruth 1:3-7

When we read the powerful account of Ruth's life, we see a much less prominent character at the beginning of her story; her sister Orpah. Orpah and Ruth had married the sons of Elimelek. Elimelek passed away leaving his wife Naomi a widow. After about ten more years, both of his sons died leaving Ruth and Orpah widows as well.

Having no more male relatives near them, they set out to the land of Judah to find Naomi's distant cousin, Boaz. Naomi urged the girls to return to their homeland and leave her, but they refused (Ruth 1:8). Again, Naomi tried to convince them to go back to their homeland and find new husbands, but they still refused.

However, the third time Naomi asked, Orpah left. Naomi said, "Look, your sister-in-law has gone back to her people and to her gods, return after your sister in law." Ruth replied, "Entreat me not to leave you, or to turn back from following after you. For wherever you go, I will go, and wherever you lodge, I will lodge. Your people shall be my people and your God, my God. Where you die, I will die and there I will be buried" (Ruth 1:15-17).

I love that passage of scripture. What a beautiful display of commitment Ruth gives us. She remained faithful to caring for her mother-in-law, while Orpah decided to leave and return to the land of her old gods.

When we are new Christians, everything is exciting and new. We feel alive and cannot wait to see what this new chapter of our lives brings us. But then, we go back to work, we go back to school, and we realize that nothing else in our lives is any different. Then, reality sets in.

We might start to question our decision. Maybe we are filled with doubts, or maybe we start to think that changing our lives is just too hard. These feelings can become overwhelming, and we might even consider giving up.

Orpah gave up. She decided it was too difficult to continue to follow Naomi back to Judah and took the easy way out. She was still young enough to get another husband, and she could live the rest of her life in the comfort of everything she knew.

The Bible doesn't mention Orpah again after she leaves. However, Ruth worked hard, remained faithful, and ended up bearing a son named Obed, who is an ancestor of Jesus himself. A widow from a strange land was found worthy of being in Jesus' lineage because of her Godly character and commitment to Naomi.

Leading a Christian life usually requires a total overhaul of our existing life. It can be a daunting task to remove things that are not helping our walk with Christ. Sometimes we have to remove friends and family members from our lives. Sometimes we have to find new hobbies or interests (because getting drunk at the local bar is no longer an option) but I can assure you that it is all worth it in the end.

God gives us the Holy Spirit to comfort us. He also gives us the freedom to find a church family to support us, and we also are blessed to have access to the Bible for encouragement when we are feeling lost. God wants the transition to be as easy as possible, and he doesn't want you to feel like you are missing out or losing something by giving your life over to him.

Don't let the devil fill your head with hesitation or self-doubt. Fully commit to God and give him control of your life. The life he has for you is better than any life you could envision yourself. God loves you so much. Stay the course and let God show you how much potential you truly have.

"You will keep him in perfect peace whose mind is stayed on you because he trusts in you. Trust in the Lord forever, for in the Lord, is everlasting strength." Isaiah 26:3-4

42

Lois and Eunice: Raising Faithful Children
2 Timothy 1:5
Proverbs 22:6

Lois and Eunice are only mentioned in one verse in the Bible. They were the grandmother and mother of Timothy and were responsible for raising him with genuine faith. This is the same faith that resided in him as an adult. He was one of Paul's followers, and he became an evangelist. Eventually, he pastored the church in Ephesus. The way Paul greeted Timothy in this scripture shows the love and respect he had for him.

Paul refers to Timothy as his son on several occasions. This indicates that Timothy may not have had a father growing up (1 Corinthians 4:17, 1 Timothy 1:18). Paul took on a fatherly role, but not until Timothy was much older. This shows us just how much influence a mother has on her children while they are still young.

These two women led a life by example and were dedicated to raising Timothy with knowledge of the scripture in hopes that he would become a man of God.

Divine Positioning for a Powerful Purpose

The Bible says to train up a child in the way he should go and when he is old, he will not depart from it (Proverbs 22:6). When our children are young, we should attempt to instill good habits in them. Praying and attending church are two ways we can apply God's Word to our children's lives.

Sheltering children too much from the world can cause more problems as it tends to leave them confused on how to navigate the world when they are grown. However, we can teach them how to handle certain situations while they are still in our homes. Bullying, drugs, alcohol, peer pressure, and sex are all common situations kids face before they graduate high school, but we can guide them through their adolescents by using the Biblical principles that God has given us.

We cannot change society over night, but we can raise children with godly character who can be trusted to make the right decisions when faced with social dilemmas. We can raise strong, independent children who will stand up to peer pressure and do the right thing as often as possible.

One of the best ways we can instill this godly character is to live the way we are asking them to live. If we are filling our day with inappropriate entertainment, cursing, and questionable friends, we can expect our children to do the same. If we are not praying, reading our Bible and attending church, our kids will not listen to us when we tell them to do those things.

Kids are resilient and adaptable. Be encouraged and know that it isn't too late to start leading like Eunice and Lois. We can change the dynamic in our relationship with our children and inspire them to lead a life after God's own heart.

"Even a child is known by his deeds. Whether what he does is pure and right." Proverbs 20:11

Reference:

1. https://teens.lovetoknow.com/Building_Resiliency_in_Adolescents

43

The Poor Widow: Giving Everything
Mark 12:41-44

When Jesus arrived in Jerusalem during Passover week, he sat in the temple and preached daily. One day, Jesus walked over to the treasury to see how the people were giving, and they were giving according to their wealth; nothing more (Mark 12:41).

Jesus noticed a poor widow with only 2 coins, and she gave both of them to the temple. She didn't do it for show. She never even saw Jesus standing there. In Mark 12:44 Jesus said, "For they all put in out of their abundance, but she out of her poverty put in all that she had, her whole livelihood."

This woman had so much faith in God that she gave all she had trusting he would provide for her. It is easy to give when we are in a season of abundance, but what about when we are struggling to make it week to week?

The Old Testament lays out a basic structure for us to tithe. The Lord requires ten percent of our total income. That is equal to one dollar out of every ten. That means he allows us to keep the other ninety percent for ourselves! God does not need our money. He already owns everything, but he established the law to test our faith.

Another part of this scripture that stands out to me is that Jesus saw her, but she didn't see him. Jesus always recognizes our giving and blesses us accordingly. When he knows he can trust us with what we are given, he will give more.

As a stay-at-home mom, I do not have an income of my own, but I am always looking for ways I can give to someone. It might be a child that needs the baseball equipment I've stored away in the closet, an elderly woman who needs a ride to the doctor, or a family that needs dinner made while they focus on making funeral arrangements for a loved one (1 Timothy 6:18).

2 Corinthians 9:7 says, "So let each one give as he purposes in his heart, not grudgingly or of necessity; for God loves a cheerful giver." If we are living a Christian life, we are to follow the example set before us through Christ and Jesus was very generous (1 John 2:6). God knows our hearts, and he wants us to give accordingly, and cheerfully.

> "Do not lay up for yourselves treasures on earth, where moth and rust destroy and where thieves break in and steal; but lay up for yourselves treasures in heaven, where neither moth nor rust destroys and where thieves do not break in and steal. For where your treasure is, there your heart will be also."
> Matthew 6:19-21

Printed in the United States
By Bookmasters